From Idea to Empire: Building a 6-Figure AI Income Stream

Scale Your AI Side Hustle Into a Global Digital Business Without Investors or Employees

By Joe Correa

Published by Live Stronger Faster

This book is for educational and informational purposes only. The author and publisher are not engaged in rendering legal, financial, or other professional advice. Readers should consult a qualified professional before making any financial decisions.

First Edition

Table of Contents

Introduction

Why Now Is the Time to Build Your AI Empire

We are in the early stages of a technological revolution unlike anything we've seen before. Artificial Intelligence is not just a buzzword—it's a business revolution, a global economic shift, and for you, a gateway to personal financial freedom. This book isn't just about making money. It's about transforming your life using AI, building something sustainable that scales globally, and doing it without investors, offices, or employees.

❖ The AI Opportunity: Why It's Exploding Right Now

Over the last few years, we've witnessed exponential growth in AI capabilities—particularly in generative AI (like ChatGPT, DALL·E, ElevenLabs, and others). These tools can now write, design, analyze, automate, and even sell for you. What once required a large team and a lot of capital can now be accomplished by a single person using the right tools and workflows.

This shift has lowered the barrier to entry for starting a high-profit business. You no longer need:

- A coding background
- A full marketing team

- Designers or video editors
- Expensive software
- Years of experience

With the right strategy and AI tools, you can go from zero to a six-figure business faster than ever before.

❖ What You'll Learn in This Book

This book gives you a step-by-step blueprint for transforming an AI side hustle into a 6-figure digital business.

You'll learn:

- How to find your AI niche with high demand and low competition
- Which AI tools save you the most time and make you the most money
- How to automate content, lead generation, and product delivery
- How to build, price, and sell AI-generated products like courses, templates, ebooks, and more
- How to create a 1-person brand that scales globally

- How to reach 6 figures without hiring or raising funds
- How to automate growth and prepare for a future sale (if you ever want to exit)

❖ Why 1-Person AI Businesses Are Outperforming Teams

We're entering the era of *solopreneur empires*—one-person businesses with global reach, full automation, and recurring revenue. These are lean, profitable, and agile businesses that don't rely on location, employees, or funding. They're run on AI tools, smart systems, and digital products.

Here's why they work:

- **Speed to market:** You can test, launch, and scale in weeks—not months.
- **Low overhead:** No payroll, office rent, or agency retainers.
- **Passive income:** AI automates fulfillment, content creation, and customer support.
- **Global reach:** Sell to anyone in the world instantly.

Even traditional startups are being replaced by solo creators using AI. Venture capital is no longer the only path to wealth.

Time freedom, control, and independence are the new markers of success.

❖ The Tools You'll Use

Throughout this book, you'll be introduced to a curated stack of no-code and AI tools that work together seamlessly. These include:

- **ChatGPT / Claude** – for content, strategy, and communication
- **ElevenLabs / Descript** – for AI voiceovers and audiobook narration
- **Invideo / Pictory / Runway** – for faceless video creation
- **Canva + Magic Studio** – for design and image generation
- **Make.com / Zapier** – for automation and backend workflows
- **Stripe / Gumroad / Payhip** – for payments and product delivery
- **Glide / Softr / Notion** – for building digital portals, SaaS MVPs, or client dashboards

You'll learn how to use these tools to create a self-operating machine—an AI-powered system that earns income while you sleep, travel, or play.

❖ Mindset Shift: From Hustle to Systems

This is not about grinding 80 hours a week to make money online. It's about *thinking like a systems builder*—someone who builds a machine once and gets paid forever.

Here's the difference:

- **Hustle Mindset:** You trade time for money, constantly chasing clients.
- **AI Empire Mindset:** You build once, automate, and scale globally.

You are not just building income streams. You're building digital assets—products, brands, and platforms—that increase in value over time.

By the end of this book, you'll have a full roadmap to go from an idea to a sustainable, scalable AI-powered empire.

Let's begin with a quick story on how Sarah went from being laid off to making $12,000 in passive income.

It started on a random Tuesday morning. Sarah sat in her

cramped kitchen, sipping instant coffee, while her two kids got ready for school. She had just been laid off—again. The tech company she worked for had slashed her department, and despite her years of loyalty, her position was deemed "nonessential." The irony wasn't lost on her. With bills piling up, no backup plan, and her confidence at an all-time low, Sarah did what most of us do in moments of desperation—she Googled "how to make money from home."

She sifted through dropshipping, affiliate marketing, survey sites, and content creation. But everything seemed saturated, scammy, or overly complicated. Then she stumbled on a Reddit thread where someone had posted: *"I made $22,000 last month using AI tools—no employees, no ads."* That single sentence lit a fire inside her. She clicked, followed the links, and discovered a world of possibilities. AI tools weren't just for tech geeks or programmers. They were being used by everyday people to build products, automate marketing, and generate income around the clock. It sounded too good to be true—but she was desperate enough to try.

Sarah began experimenting with ChatGPT to help her write blog content. Within a few hours, she had created three full blog posts. Then she used Canva and DALL·E to generate custom images for each one. For voiceovers, she tried ElevenLabs and was stunned at how real the AI voices sounded. The next week, she created her first digital product—an ebook titled *"AI Tools for Busy Moms"*—and uploaded it to Gumroad. She priced it at $9.99, unsure if anyone would buy. Within 48 hours, she had her first sale. Then five. Then twenty. Each time her phone pinged with a new sale, it felt like a tiny miracle.

Sarah quickly realized that the key wasn't creating one product—it was building a system. She set up an email list using MailerLite and connected it to a landing page built with Notion. She used Make.com to automate her welcome emails, upsells, and thank-you messages. She started recording short-form videos using Invideo, sharing tips on how other moms could do the same. Those videos began to go viral. Her followers grew. Her email list exploded. Her $9.99 ebook turned into a $29 bundle, then a $97 course—all created using AI tools, all automated from start to finish.

Six months after her layoff, Sarah was earning over $12,000 per month in passive income. She had no office, no staff, no inventory, and no ad spend. Just a laptop, some AI tools, and a drive to never be financially dependent on anyone again. Her AI-powered business wasn't just profitable—it was liberating. She could work during school hours and be fully present for her kids in the afternoons. She no longer worried about job security or begging for raises. She was building an empire—on her own terms.

What surprised Sarah the most wasn't the money—it was how simple it all was once she got started. She didn't need to be tech-savvy. She didn't need funding. She didn't even need to leave her house. The tools did most of the work. All she had to do was string them together, build once, and let the system run.

Sarah's story isn't an outlier—it's becoming the norm. Across the world, people are realizing they can build high-leverage businesses without a team, a boss, or a giant budget. They're using AI to do the heavy lifting and keeping the profits for themselves. And just like Sarah, you can do it too. You don't need to know everything now. You just need to be willing to take the first step.

That's what this book is here for. To give you a clear, simple roadmap—from the moment the idea hits, to the day you check your dashboard and realize you've built something that runs while you sleep. Sarah's journey is proof. Now it's your turn.

Chapter 1: Finding Your Profitable AI Niche

The first and most important step in building a profitable AI-powered business is identifying a niche. A niche is a specific market segment with a unique need or problem that you can solve with your AI tools, content, or digital products. It's the foundation for everything you'll build—from the products you offer to the audience you serve, the content you create, and how you market your brand. If you try to appeal to everyone, you'll end up resonating with no one. But if you pick a narrow, high-demand niche, your business can grow rapidly—without spending much on ads or trying to compete in oversaturated spaces.

A profitable AI niche lies at the intersection of three things: your interests or skills, growing market demand, and monetizable problems. You don't need to be an expert, but you do need to be interested enough to create valuable content and solutions consistently. Think about what excites you: Is it real estate, fitness, career advancement, education, parenting, mental health, or small business? Then, explore how AI can enhance those areas. For example, if you're interested in fitness, you could create an AI-generated personalized workout planner or meal plan tool. If you're into career growth, you could build resume generators, interview prep bots, or LinkedIn profile optimizers.

Start by brainstorming your top five interests, skills, or industries you understand. Then ask: "What AI-enhanced solution would people in this space pay for?" The goal is to solve a problem faster, easier, or cheaper using AI. Use tools like Google Trends, Reddit forums, YouTube search suggestions, and Amazon product reviews to identify pain points in your niche. Don't just look at what people are buying—look at what they're complaining about. Frustrations often lead to purchases. For example, if people complain about the time it takes to edit videos, that's a clue you could offer AI video editing services or a prebuilt automation template using tools like Runway or Pictory.

Once you've identified 2–3 potential niches, validate them. Use platforms like Gumroad, Etsy, Udemy, and YouTube to search for products, digital tools, or content in that niche. Are there creators making money? Are their products getting reviews and comments? Is there demand but not overwhelming saturation? If yes, you're in the right place. Better yet, search on TikTok, Instagram Reels, and YouTube Shorts for trends—short videos often reveal rising niches before they hit mainstream marketplaces.

It's also helpful to look at communities. Join Facebook groups, Discord servers, or Reddit threads in your niche. Watch how people talk. What do they need help with? What are the most common questions? You'll start to see patterns. These patterns are clues to build your product and content strategy. If everyone is asking how to make money with AI in real estate, for example, that's a huge signal. You could create an AI-powered property analysis tool, a real estate chatbot, or a course on AI automation for brokers.

The key is to avoid broad, vague niches like "make money online" or "health." Instead, go deeper: "AI tools for Etsy shop owners," "AI automation for mortgage brokers," or "AI content creation for fitness influencers." The more specific your niche, the easier it is to dominate and scale quickly. You can always expand later—but domination starts with focus.

Lastly, remember this: you don't need a revolutionary idea. You just need to solve a real problem with an AI-enhanced solution in a space you care about. Your niche doesn't have to be perfect—it just has to be clear, profitable, and growing. And once it is, the next chapters will show you how to turn that idea into an automated, income-producing empire.

The AI-Powered Etsy Product

Carlos had always been a tech enthusiast, but he never saw himself as an entrepreneur. He worked as an IT technician at a local school district and spent most of his evenings gaming or tinkering with his custom-built PC. He followed the rise of artificial intelligence with interest, occasionally testing new apps or reading about breakthroughs in natural language processing. But it wasn't until a casual conversation with his cousin that he considered using AI to start a business.

His cousin Sofia was a small business owner who ran an Etsy shop selling handmade planners. Over lunch, she vented about how much time she spent rewriting product descriptions, creating social media posts, and responding to customer questions. "If only I had a robot that could do this," she joked. Carlos laughed, but a lightbulb went off. He realized he did know how to create that robot—or at least assemble the tools to mimic one. That night, Carlos opened ChatGPT and experimented with writing Etsy product descriptions using prompts tailored to handmade planners. The results were fast and surprisingly good.

The next day, he listed a gig on Fiverr offering "AI-Powered Etsy Product Descriptions – Delivered in 24 Hours." He priced it at $15. To his surprise, a seller ordered the same day. She loved the results. Then another. Soon, Carlos had repeat clients and referrals. But the real shift came when he realized he could package this as a product, not just a service. He created a Google Sheet template with built-in prompts and a Notion guide that taught Etsy sellers how to use AI to automate their own product listings, descriptions, hashtags, and even customer responses.

Carlos started researching other pain points in the Etsy space. He joined Facebook groups and noticed a recurring complaint: content creation was exhausting and time-consuming. Many sellers were moms or creatives, not tech-savvy marketers. They didn't want to learn about SEO—they just wanted more sales. So Carlos created a simple AI prompt pack for Etsy success. He bundled it with a 20-minute Loom tutorial and uploaded the digital product to Gumroad. The price? $19. Within two weeks, he had 53 sales—all from organic traffic and word of mouth.

Still, he wondered if this niche was too narrow. He dabbled in other ideas—AI for teachers, AI for gamers, AI for YouTubers. But every time he ventured out, he came back to Etsy sellers. That niche was underserved, passionate, and hungry for solutions. He realized that being specific wasn't a limitation—it was a superpower. He didn't need to be the best AI expert in the world. He just needed to be the best at solving one clear problem for one specific group of people.

He doubled down. Carlos launched an AI automation toolkit specifically for Etsy businesses. He used Make.com to automate email responses, Canva to generate social media content, and Pictory to produce simple promotional videos for his landing page. He shared tips on TikTok, posted free prompts in Etsy seller groups, and invited feedback from his customers to improve the product. Within three months, he had built a $4,000/month digital income stream—all based on a niche he discovered during a family lunch.

Carlos's story is a reminder that great business ideas aren't always born from boardrooms or brainstorms. Sometimes, they come from solving someone else's everyday problem. And the riches aren't in being broad—they're in being specific. AI didn't just give Carlos a toolkit. It gave him a way to build something real, scalable, and entirely his own—starting from nothing more than curiosity and a conversation.

Chapter 2: AI Tools That Build Your Business for You

Once you've chosen a profitable niche, the next step is to build your AI toolkit. This isn't just about choosing flashy software—it's about creating a lean, integrated stack of tools that can automate, enhance, and scale your business without adding complexity. The goal is to turn your idea into an income-producing machine by offloading time-consuming tasks to AI. Whether you're creating digital products, services, or content, the right tools will allow you to act like a full team of writers, designers, marketers, editors, and support reps—all by yourself.

Let's start with content creation. At the core of your business will likely be written content—product descriptions, blog posts, video scripts, social media captions, sales pages, and email sequences. For this, nothing beats ChatGPT or Claude. These large language models can write engaging, human-like text on virtually any topic, in any tone, and for any platform. Learn to craft strong prompts that give the AI context, audience, structure, and intent. Save your best prompts in a prompt library and reuse them across projects. For example, a single "AI sales page generator" prompt can be used for every new digital product you launch.

Next, consider voice and video. If you're planning to create audiobooks, faceless YouTube videos, or voiceover-led courses, use tools like ElevenLabs, Descript, or PlayHT. These platforms allow you to generate high-quality audio using AI voices that sound natural and professional. For video, tools like Invideo, Pictory, and Runway let you create and edit videos without showing your face, recording anything, or hiring editors. You simply drop in your script and media, and the platform does the rest. These tools are perfect for short-form content (TikToks, Reels, Shorts) or long-form explainers.

Design and visuals are next. Canva, especially when paired with Magic Studio or DALL·E, lets you generate stunning graphics, ebook covers, thumbnails, presentations, and templates in minutes. You can now automate design workflows using Canva's Magic Resize, Magic Write, and AI-powered suggestions. If you're building digital downloads like planners, templates, or slide decks, Canva should be your go-to tool. It replaces the need for Photoshop, InDesign, or freelance designers.

Now let's talk automation. This is where your business becomes hands-free. Tools like Make.com, Zapier, and Airtable allow you to connect different platforms so tasks happen without you lifting a finger. For example, when a customer buys your ebook on Gumroad, an automation can send them a thank-you email, grant access to a Notion course portal, add them to your email list, and trigger a follow-up sequence—all without you touching a thing. This is where your 1-person business truly becomes scalable. Set it up once and let the automations run 24/7.

For sales and product delivery, use platforms like Stripe, Gumroad, Payhip, LemonSqueezy, or Sellfy. These tools let you collect payments, offer upsells, host files, and deliver your product instantly. You don't need a custom website to start. These platforms give you a hosted checkout page, email collection, customer dashboard, and analytics. You can even use them to host memberships, subscriptions, or limited-time offers. Combine this with link-in-bio tools like Solo.to or Beacons to unify your brand presence.

If you're building something more interactive—like an AI-powered tool, a digital dashboard, or a no-code SaaS—use Glide, Notion, Softr, or Tally. These platforms let you build beautiful front-end experiences without code. For example, you can turn an Airtable database into a client-facing web app with Glide, create a paid resource hub with Notion, or build a quiz-based product selector with Tally and embed it on your Gumroad sales page. These tools give your business depth and interactivity with zero coding.

Don't get overwhelmed by all the options. You only need a few key tools to begin. Start with a simple stack: ChatGPT for writing, Canva for visuals, ElevenLabs for voice, Pictory for video, Make.com for automation, and Gumroad for selling. As your business grows, you can add layers of complexity and customization. But remember: simplicity scales. The more streamlined your toolkit, the more repeatable and efficient your systems will be.

The real power lies in combining these tools into workflows. For example: AI writes your blog > AI turns it into a video > AI voices the script > AI posts it to Instagram and YouTube > automation sends new leads to your sales funnel. You become a content-producing, product-selling machine powered by smart workflows instead of human labor.

With the right AI stack in place, you can finally stop trading time for money and start building something that grows on autopilot. In the next chapter, you'll learn how to turn this toolkit into a functioning system that runs whether you're working, sleeping, or on vacation.

Nina's digital product idea

Nina was a freelance copywriter who had grown tired of chasing invoices and juggling ten different clients every month. She loved writing, but the constant pressure to meet deadlines, revise drafts, and stay on top of client expectations left her burned out. What she craved wasn't just more money—it was freedom. She wanted to build something once and let it work for her. She wanted to stop trading hours for dollars. One night, while watching a YouTube video on side hustles, she discovered the world of AI automation.

At first, Nina was skeptical. She had heard of ChatGPT but assumed it was just another gimmicky writing tool. But curiosity got the better of her. She signed up and started playing with prompts. Within 30 minutes, she had created a full blog post, a newsletter, and a video script. The quality blew her away. It wasn't perfect, but it was fast—and with her editing skills, it was good enough to publish. That was the moment something shifted. If she could produce in one hour what used to take three, maybe she could finally scale without burnout.

The next day, Nina mapped out a digital product idea: a guided journaling template for creatives. She used ChatGPT to write the prompts and reflection questions, then brought the content into Canva to design a beautiful, printable layout. With Canva's Magic Resize, she repurposed the layout for Instagram posts and Pinterest pins. Then, she recorded a short voiceover for the product trailer using ElevenLabs. The entire process—from idea to finished product—took her under two days. She uploaded the journal to Payhip and made her first sale a few hours later. It was only $7, but the ping on her phone felt like freedom.

Encouraged by the response, Nina built a second product: a mini-course on using AI to speed up writing. She used Descript to record and edit a faceless video series, then used Pictory to slice the long video into short-form clips for Instagram and TikTok. She connected her Gumroad sales page to Make.com so that each purchase would trigger a welcome email, unlock the course materials in Notion, and tag the customer in her mailing list. For the first time ever, Nina had a system that ran while she slept.

She was stunned by how much time she reclaimed. What used to take a week—writing, editing, designing, promoting—now took hours. The AI tools didn't just help her create faster; they gave her space to think bigger. Instead of freelancing just to survive, she could now focus on building. Each week, she created new assets: AI prompt packs for authors, visual quote templates, content calendars—all of it powered by ChatGPT, Canva, and her growing skill in automation. Her followers grew. Her email list expanded. Her sales multiplied.

Eventually, Nina stopped taking freelance clients altogether. Her monthly passive income had surpassed her previous full-time earnings. What amazed her most wasn't the money—it was the realization that she had built a business without hiring anyone, without launching ads, and without spending more than $50 on software. Her "team" was a stack of AI tools that worked 24/7, never complained, and didn't need lunch breaks. And best of all, she still had time to write—for herself.

Nina's story is proof that the tools are already here. You don't need a huge budget, a fancy degree, or a tech background. You just need a clear idea and the right stack. With the power of AI, she went from freelancer to founder, from chasing clients to creating freedom—all by letting the tools do the heavy lifting. And if she could do it, starting from a single product and a weekend of curiosity, so can you.

Chapter 3: From Side Hustle to System: Setting Up Your AI Automation Stack

Once you've selected your niche and assembled your AI toolkit, the next step is to set up an automated business system. This is where your side hustle turns into a scalable machine. Many entrepreneurs get stuck in the trap of constant output—writing, designing, recording, responding—without realizing that 90% of those tasks can be automated or semi-automated using AI and no-code tools. The goal here is to work once, automate the rest, and create a business that earns around the clock, whether you're online or not.

To begin, you need to define your core offer. This could be a digital product like an ebook, course, template bundle, or AI prompt pack. Or it could be a service enhanced by automation—such as AI resume writing or personalized nutrition plans. Once your offer is created, the system you build around it needs to do four things: attract leads, convert them into buyers, deliver the product, and nurture the relationship afterward. When each of these parts is automated, you're no longer stuck inside the business—you're overseeing the system.

The first part of your automation stack is **lead capture**. You want to collect emails from visitors in exchange for a free value offer—often called a lead magnet. This could be a mini-guide, cheat sheet, checklist, or free training. Use a simple landing page builder like ConvertKit, MailerLite, or Notion in combination with a form tool like Tally. Once someone opts in, your email platform should automatically send a welcome sequence that delivers the freebie, introduces your paid offer, and includes call-to-action links to buy. All of this can be built once and reused for every future product.

Next is **content automation**. This includes using AI to create blog posts, social media content, and short-form videos that drive traffic to your funnel. Tools like ChatGPT and Claude can generate content calendars, write carousels, and script your Reels or Shorts. You can schedule this content using Buffer or Metricool. Video tools like Invideo or Pictory can turn blog posts into videos with AI-generated voiceovers and captions. Then you distribute them automatically across YouTube Shorts, Instagram, and TikTok to grow your audience without constantly creating from scratch.

Now comes **sales and fulfillment**. When someone buys, your payment processor (like Gumroad, Stripe, or Payhip) should immediately trigger a series of automations. These include sending a purchase confirmation, granting access to the product (via Google Drive, Notion, or a membership site), adding the buyer to a segmented email list, and sending follow-up upsell offers. You can build these workflows using Make.com or Zapier to connect your payment platform to your delivery platform and email service. That means zero manual work after the sale—every buyer gets their content instantly, and every upsell is delivered without your involvement.

Don't forget **customer relationship automation**. The long-term value of your business comes from your list—not just one-time buyers. Use automated surveys (Google Forms, Tally, or Typeform) to collect feedback and testimonials. Schedule pre-written emails that check in with your customers after 7, 14, or 30 days. You can even automate loyalty bonuses, birthday offers, or milestone gifts using tools like Make.com connected to Airtable or Google Sheets. The key is to make your customers feel like you're always there—even when you're not.

Finally, **track your data automatically**. Use Notion or Google Sheets as your dashboard. Pull in sales data, email opt-ins, and audience growth using connected tools or integrations. Check this dashboard weekly to identify which funnels, products, or content are performing best. That insight allows you to double down on what's working and tweak what's not. The more you refine, the more powerful and passive your system becomes.

The beauty of an AI automation stack is that it doesn't require expensive developers or months of planning. You can build version one in a weekend. And as you grow, you just layer on new automations or upgrade individual tools. This is how one-person businesses scale to six figures without hiring a team. You're not building a hustle. You're building a system. One that runs on code, content, and creativity—powered by AI.

Jasmine's fully automated digital business

Jasmine never intended to start a business. She was a part-time marketing assistant and full-time mom who dabbled in journaling and digital planning during her limited free time. One evening, while watching her toddler play on the floor, she noticed a YouTube ad for a free workshop on AI-powered side hustles. Out of curiosity, she signed up. What started as a 60-minute session became a total mind shift. Jasmine realized she didn't need more time—she needed a smarter system.

She began by creating a simple digital product: a 30-day guided gratitude journal with prompts generated by ChatGPT. She used Canva to design it and uploaded it to Gumroad for sale. To promote it, she created a free 5-day version and offered it in exchange for an email address. She used ConvertKit to set up her opt-in form and welcome sequence. When someone signed up, they received an email with the freebie, a short story about her own gratitude journey, and an invitation to buy the full version. It all felt simple—because it was. And the best part? She only had to set it up once.

At first, she managed the emails manually. But as her subscriber list grew past 300, she decided to automate the entire process. She linked Gumroad to Make.com and built a workflow: whenever someone purchased the journal, they automatically received a download link, were added to her "customers" list, tagged as a buyer, and sent a thank-you email. She no longer had to lift a finger. Then she added another automation: after 7 days, buyers received a "how's it going?" message with a link to leave a review. After 14 days, they got a surprise discount for her next product—a journaling prompt deck. That one workflow doubled her repeat customers in two weeks.

Jasmine also wanted to grow her audience through content. But with two kids under five, time was limited. So she leaned on automation. She asked ChatGPT to write 30 short affirmations and quotes. Then, she pasted them into Canva using bulk creation and generated a month's worth of Instagram posts. Using Metricool, she scheduled the content to auto-post daily. She also created short voiceover videos using Pictory and ElevenLabs. Her follower count grew. People started DMing her to ask about the journal. Every day, new leads entered her funnel without her having to create anything new.

She kept going. Jasmine built a Notion dashboard where she tracked her weekly sales, email subscribers, and top-performing posts. She pulled in data using Make.com so she didn't have to log into ten different tools. Her Sunday night "CEO hour" was now just reviewing one page and making small tweaks. Over time, she noticed which lead magnets converted best, which videos got the most clicks, and which emails led to the most purchases. That insight allowed her to optimize faster than she ever imagined.

Six months in, Jasmine had built a fully automated digital business around her lifestyle. She spent only five hours a week maintaining it—usually while her kids napped or played. Her income surpassed $5,000 per month, and more importantly, she finally felt present in her life again. She wasn't scrambling or glued to her phone. Her business ran like a machine, freeing her to be a mother, a creator, and an entrepreneur on her own terms.

What Jasmine built wasn't magic. It was a system. Piece by piece, she used AI and automation to replace manual work with smart workflows. No employees. No burnout. Just repeatable actions, running quietly in the background. Her story is a testament to the power of stacking small, automated steps into a business that scales. If she could do it in the cracks of her day—with no tech background—so can you.

Chapter 4: Content, Courses, and Cash Flow: Products That Sell Themselves

Now that your systems are in place, it's time to focus on creating income-generating products—digital assets that sell themselves repeatedly with little to no maintenance. This chapter is all about turning your niche knowledge, AI tools, and automation stack into tangible content, digital courses, and cash-flowing assets that customers can purchase at any time from anywhere in the world. The magic of AI is not just in creation—it's in turning what you know (or what AI can help you structure) into a product that pays you over and over again without additional effort.

Let's begin with content. Your first goal is to build authority and attract attention through free value content. This includes blog posts, email newsletters, Instagram carousels, TikTok clips, YouTube Shorts, and lead magnets. Use AI to batch-create content around your niche. Start by giving ChatGPT 10 pain points your audience faces. Then ask it to create hooks, headlines, captions, scripts, and even call-to-action prompts. If you want to move fast, use a prompt library to create 30 days of content in under two hours. Content builds trust—and trust sells products.

Once your content machine is running, turn it into products.

The easiest path is to start with downloadable digital products: ebooks, guides, templates, checklists, AI prompt packs, planners, and toolkits. These items solve small but specific problems. For example, if you help fitness coaches, create a "30 ChatGPT Prompts to Automate Your Fitness Content" bundle. Use Canva to format, ChatGPT to generate the content, and Gumroad or Payhip to sell it. With AI, you can create and publish a product in 48 hours or less.

After that, level up to courses. These don't need to be long, polished video series. In fact, you can build entire mini-courses using slides, screen recordings, or even voiceover walk-throughs. A 30-minute course that solves a real problem can earn more than a 3-hour one that doesn't. Use ChatGPT to outline lessons, write scripts, and even generate visual examples or case studies. Tools like Tella, Loom, or Descript make recording your course fast and simple—especially when paired with AI-generated slides or Notion-based content hubs.

Remember, your product doesn't have to be based solely on your expertise. AI can help you research, organize, and even write your course or ebook. What matters most is that the final product delivers results. If you combine your experience, AI's power, and a clear transformation for the buyer, your product will have value. Add bonuses like templates, checklists, or case studies to increase perceived value. Then use automation to upsell these assets after a customer's first purchase.

To generate cash flow consistently, use pricing strategies that work with your funnel. Start with a low-ticket front-end product (under $30) to drive volume and build trust. Then offer a higher-value bundle or course ($97–$197) once someone is on your list. Use automation to trigger upsells, limited-time discounts, and reminders based on behavior. Your funnel should run 24/7, making sales even while you sleep.

Offer variety in how your content is consumed. Convert your ebook into an audiobook using ElevenLabs or PlayHT. Turn your checklist into a Canva template. Use your blog content to build a Notion course hub. Every digital asset you create can be repurposed into a second, third, or fourth format—each one giving you another income stream. The more formats you offer, the more buyers you'll convert based on their preferences.

Test everything. The first product won't be perfect—but that's okay. The key is speed and feedback. Launch a minimal viable version, collect reviews, improve it, and relaunch. AI helps you iterate fast. Use Make.com to automate review collection or post-sale surveys. Over time, you'll build a portfolio of digital products that consistently convert and deliver value to your audience.

By turning your AI-enhanced content into courses, templates, and tools, you move from creator to business owner. You're no longer just publishing for fun—you're selling assets that generate freedom. The next chapter will show you how to drive leads to those products automatically, using AI-powered marketing strategies that grow your brand and income exponentially.

How Marcus profited from his mini-course

Marcus had always been good at explaining things. As a former middle school science teacher, he had a knack for breaking down complex topics into clear, engaging lessons. After leaving the classroom during the pandemic, he began posting short educational videos on TikTok to stay sharp and possibly earn some side income. He never imagined it would turn into something much bigger. At first, his videos were simple: "Why the sky is blue," "How photosynthesis works," "What is quantum entanglement?" He used ChatGPT to help him write concise scripts and Canva to add simple animations. Within two months, one of his clips went viral. Thousands of new followers poured in overnight, and many asked the same question: "Do you have a course I can buy?"

That question planted the seed. Marcus hadn't thought of himself as a course creator, but clearly there was demand. He asked ChatGPT to help him outline a course titled *Everyday Science Explained: 10 Concepts That Will Blow Your Mind.* He used a Google Doc to organize the lessons, then recorded short 5-minute videos using Loom, walking through slides he built in Canva. He didn't even use his face—just screen shares and voiceovers. In less than a week, he had a complete mini-course and uploaded it to Gumroad for $29. He made three sales on day one. By the end of the week, he had 48 sales. The income was great—but what surprised him more was the feedback. People loved his teaching style, the simplicity, and the clarity.

That success gave Marcus momentum. He turned his scripts into a digital workbook using Notion. Then he recorded an audiobook version of the course using ElevenLabs. Without realizing it, he now had three products from the same original content: a video course, a digital workbook, and an audiobook. He bundled them into a $97 premium version and added a bonus "AI prompt guide for educators," which he created in a single afternoon with ChatGPT. That bundle became his best-seller and accounted for 70% of his income.

To scale further, Marcus began posting content consistently—daily videos on TikTok and Instagram, all created in batches using AI tools. He used Metricool to schedule his posts and made sure each one had a strong call-to-action: "Link in bio for the full course." He also created a free email course using ConvertKit—a 3-day mini science lesson series delivered automatically to new subscribers. This funnel fed into his $29 course, and later, his $97 bundle. He added automation so that if someone clicked but didn't buy, they received a reminder email with a time-limited coupon. His sales jumped 35% after implementing this one feature.

By month five, Marcus was earning over $6,000 per month—entirely from digital products. No customer service headaches. No ad spend. No inventory. Just helpful content powered by AI, distributed through social platforms, and delivered through smart systems. What started as curiosity had become a full-fledged digital business.

Marcus didn't have a massive audience, a flashy website, or a complex tech stack. What he had was clarity. He knew who he was serving, what problems he was solving, and how to deliver that value through formats people wanted. He focused on the essentials: content that educates, products that solve, and systems that sell. AI made it all faster. Automation made it effortless. And his story is proof that with a few smart tools and the right mindset, anyone can turn their knowledge into cash flow.

Chapter 5: Lead Generation on Autopilot with AI

No matter how great your digital product is, it won't make you money unless people know it exists. That's why lead generation is the engine of your AI-powered business. The goal isn't just traffic—it's quality leads: people who are interested in your niche, see value in your offer, and are willing to spend money. In the digital age, attention is currency. But with AI, you don't need to chase leads or manually hustle on every platform. You can build lead systems that operate 24/7, attract ideal buyers, and automatically feed your funnel without paid ads or constant posting.

The foundation of lead generation is content, but not just random posts. You need intentional content that attracts, educates, and converts. Use ChatGPT to create short-form scripts optimized for virality: 15 to 60-second clips with a hook, value, and CTA. Turn these scripts into Reels, Shorts, and TikToks using Invideo, Pictory, or Canva's video editor. Batch record or generate 10–20 videos at a time and schedule them across platforms using Metricool or Buffer. Every video should end with a call to action: "Get the free guide," "Join my free email course," or "Download the free checklist"—all of which lead back to your lead magnet landing page.

Your lead magnet is your most important conversion tool. It should be specific, fast to consume, and immediately valuable. Examples include AI prompt packs, cheat sheets, mini-courses, templates, or audio downloads. Create them with ChatGPT and Canva, then deliver them through email platforms like ConvertKit, MailerLite, or Flodesk. Set up automations so that as soon as someone opts in, they receive a series of emails: the first delivering the freebie, and the rest introducing your products. These emails don't have to be fancy—just helpful, honest, and direct, using AI to write or edit them efficiently.

Don't stop with one platform. Multiply your reach. Repurpose your content across multiple channels. A YouTube Short becomes an Instagram Reel, a TikTok clip, and a LinkedIn post. Your lead magnet landing page link should be in every bio and mentioned in every caption. Use Solo.to or Beacons to create a mobile-optimized link hub that connects all your offers, freebies, and channels in one place. With AI-generated content and smart scheduling, you'll stay visible without being constantly online.

AI can also help you with SEO-based lead generation. Use ChatGPT to generate blog posts targeting long-tail keywords in your niche. Tools like NeuronWriter or Surfer SEO can help optimize content structure. Once published, use Make.com to automate sharing across platforms or notify your email list. Even one well-ranked article can drive hundreds of leads a month—passively. Pair this with Pinterest pins (generated with Canva and AI titles), and you can build a long-term traffic system with zero ad spend.

To further automate your lead flow, use quizzes or diagnostic tools. Tally and Typeform allow you to build "What kind of X are you?" quizzes that segment your leads and recommend the right product. Pair this with AI copy and logic flows, and you've built a gamified lead magnet that's fun, viral, and effective. You can even integrate quiz answers with your email platform to send personalized emails based on the results. This boosts open rates, click-throughs, and conversions dramatically.

Make sure to track everything. Use a Notion or Airtable dashboard to monitor how many leads you're getting daily, where they're coming from, and which ones convert. Over time, you'll discover your highest-performing traffic sources and lead magnets. Then you double down on what works and prune what doesn't. This iterative feedback loop is what turns slow growth into a steady snowball effect.

Finally, always lead with value. The best lead generation is rooted in service—genuinely helping people before asking for anything in return. If your content solves problems, your lead magnet delivers quick wins, and your product is the natural next step, your audience will thank you with attention—and with purchases. With AI and automation on your side, your lead generation becomes a system, not a struggle. And once that system is running smoothly, scaling your income becomes inevitable.

Tyler's social media experience

Tyler had been selling a $27 AI prompt pack for real estate agents for three weeks. He made a few sales through word of mouth and a couple of posts in Facebook groups, but the results were inconsistent. Some days he had two sales, other days zero. He knew he had a great product—he just didn't have a consistent way to get people to see it. At first, he thought about running ads, but the idea of burning through money without knowing what worked made him hesitate. That's when he stumbled onto a YouTube video titled "How I Built a Free AI Lead Machine That Runs Itself." He clicked play—and everything changed.

The creator explained how to use ChatGPT to write viral video scripts, use Invideo to create short-form videos, and schedule everything using Metricool. Tyler took notes. That night, he asked ChatGPT to write ten scripts that answered questions real estate agents might Google: "How to use AI to write a listing description," "AI tools that replace your assistant," "How to save 10 hours a week as an agent." He edited the scripts slightly, dropped them into Invideo, added a few icons and music, and scheduled them across TikTok, YouTube Shorts, and Instagram Reels. Each one ended with a line: "Get the free AI cheat sheet for realtors—link in bio."

But he didn't have a cheat sheet yet—so he made one. It took him less than two hours using ChatGPT and Canva. He created a lead magnet called "The 10 Best AI Prompts Every Realtor Needs" and connected it to a MailerLite landing page. When someone downloaded it, they were added to an email sequence he wrote using AI. The first email delivered the freebie, the second introduced his paid prompt pack, and the third offered a time-limited discount. He wrote all three emails with ChatGPT and set them up to run automatically.

Within a few days, he started seeing email signups from his short videos. Then came sales. His list went from 0 to 500 in three weeks—all organically. One of his TikToks crossed 40,000 views. A real estate influencer reposted it. His MailerLite dashboard lit up like a Christmas tree. And the best part? He wasn't manually messaging anyone or running cold outreach. It was all running in the background while he focused on creating better offers and tweaking his funnel.

Tyler's next move was SEO. He wrote five blog posts using ChatGPT and optimized them for keywords like "AI for real estate marketing" and "best AI tools for realtors." He posted them to his Notion site and shared them across his social media. He used Canva to create Pinterest pins for each blog post and scheduled them to go out over the next month. He wasn't a Pinterest expert, but he didn't have to be. The AI helped him format titles, craft descriptions, and build simple infographics that looked great.

Then he built a quiz. Using Tally, he created "What Kind of AI-Enhanced Agent Are You?"—a 7-question personality quiz that segmented realtors into four types and recommended a specific product bundle at the end. People loved it. They shared their results, forwarded it to friends, and clicked the links. Tyler connected Tally to MailerLite so every quiz taker got personalized follow-up emails based on their result. His open and click-through rates shot up.

By month two, Tyler had grown his list to over 1,800 subscribers. His AI prompt pack was generating $3,000/month in sales—and he hadn't spent a dollar on ads. His videos kept working, his blog posts were ranking, and his quiz continued to generate leads like clockwork. He had finally escaped the feast-or-famine cycle of inconsistent sales.

Looking back, Tyler realized the key wasn't just creating a good product—it was building a lead machine. AI gave him the tools to write faster, design quicker, and automate smarter. He didn't need to be a marketing genius. He just needed to connect the dots: content that helped, a freebie that converted, and a system that followed up. His business didn't just grow—it started to scale. And it all began the day he stopped chasing leads and let AI bring them to him.

Chapter 6: Monetizing With Minimalism: No Office, No Team, No Problem

The old model of business was built on complexity—offices, employees, meetings, managers, and endless layers of structure. But in today's AI-driven economy, lean is powerful. You no longer need a big team or a fancy office to earn big. In fact, the most profitable AI businesses today are often run by just one person with a clear product, a few smart systems, and a minimalist mindset. This chapter is all about simplifying your business structure while maximizing your income. The goal is freedom, not busywork. You're not trying to look impressive—you're building a system that earns without chaos.

Start with your workspace. You don't need a rented office or a stack of monitors. A laptop, a phone, and internet access are all you truly need. Use Notion as your business HQ. Build dashboards to track your income, projects, ideas, customer feedback, and growth metrics. Create shared databases to store AI prompts, content libraries, and product roadmaps. Notion replaces dozens of apps in one place, saving you time and mental load.

Next, simplify your communication. Since you don't have a

team, eliminate internal meetings altogether. Use tools like Tella or Loom to record updates for yourself or future collaborators. These tools are also perfect for training videos, product tutorials, and customer onboarding content. One recording can serve hundreds of customers or future hires without needing your time again. Think asynchronous and evergreen whenever possible.

For customer service, use AI to cut out 90% of the work. Create an FAQ using ChatGPT, then turn it into a chatbot with tools like Tidio, Intercom, or Chatbase. You can embed this chatbot on your product pages, course platforms, or landing pages to answer questions instantly. For email support, use canned responses generated by AI that address common issues like login help, refunds, or product access. Most customer interactions are repetitive—so automate the responses and reclaim your time.

When it comes to operations, minimalism means using as few tools as possible—and making sure they integrate. Stick to platforms that do more than one thing. Gumroad, for example, handles payment, product hosting, email collection, and customer analytics. Canva is great for design, presentations, and even social media scheduling. ConvertKit does email and landing pages. Make.com connects all your apps together. You don't need dozens of tools—you need a reliable few that talk to each other and run in the background.

Avoid the temptation to outsource everything too early. Many people rush to hire VAs or freelancers, thinking it will save time. But more people means more management, more instructions, and more mental clutter. Instead, challenge yourself to see what AI can replace first. Before hiring a copywriter, try ChatGPT. Before hiring a video editor, try Pictory. Before hiring a customer support agent, try a chatbot. You'll often find the task gets done faster, cheaper, and more consistently—without adding a new person to manage.

Schedule your work around high-leverage activities only. Use a weekly "CEO day" to review your sales dashboard, content metrics, and automation performance. Identify bottlenecks, fix friction points, and create systems to solve them. Spend 80% of your time building products, content, and systems that earn passively. Avoid tasks that don't directly produce revenue or growth unless they're fully automated. A minimalist business is focused, not scattered.

Financially, keep your expenses lean. Avoid software bloat, tool duplication, and unnecessary subscriptions. Track monthly costs inside Notion or a simple Google Sheet. Calculate your income-to-effort ratio every month. If a product or system brings in revenue with minimal effort, double down.

If it requires frequent manual work, either automate it or cut it. Profitability isn't about more effort—it's about more leverage.

Ultimately, monetizing with minimalism means building a business that gives you time freedom, location freedom, and mental clarity. AI and automation let you reduce noise while increasing income. You don't need an empire to look like an empire. You just need a streamlined machine that runs efficiently and quietly behind the scenes. In the next chapter, we'll explore how to use this lean structure to build a global brand from home.

The Solopreneur's AI Toolkit

Lena never liked the idea of managing people. She had worked in corporate operations for years and knew how quickly a team could turn from an asset into a liability. Meetings, drama, sick days, personality clashes—it drained her. So, when she left her job to build something of her own, she made herself a promise: no office, no staff, no overhead. She wanted freedom, not complexity. At first, she didn't even consider herself an entrepreneur. She just wanted to make enough to cover her rent, buy herself time, and stop checking her email obsessively every morning.

She started simple. Lena created a $17 digital guide called *The Solopreneur's AI Toolkit*, a collection of prompt templates, tools, and automations she had used to stay productive and save time. She used Canva to design the guide, Notion to organize her process, and Gumroad to sell it. The first week, she made 14 sales from a single post on Reddit. Encouraged, she built a landing page with ConvertKit, offered a free "5 AI Hacks for Productivity" lead magnet, and wrote three automated emails using ChatGPT. Her funnel was simple, clean, and effective. Within a month, she had 500 email subscribers and was earning over $1,000/month—no ads, no sales calls, and no team.

But what really changed everything was when she asked, "What else can I remove?" She realized that most of her energy went into repetitive tasks: responding to questions, posting updates, checking orders. So, she started stripping things down. She used ChatGPT to build a detailed FAQ and turned it into a chatbot using Chatbase. Now, visitors to her site could get instant help, 24/7. She recorded a single 3-minute Loom video that welcomed buyers, walked them through the product, and answered common questions—no more support emails. She scheduled all her content using Metricool in weekly batches, so her social media ran on autopilot while she worked (or rested).

Her workspace was even simpler. A laptop, headphones, Notion, and two browser tabs open at a time. She created a Notion dashboard to manage her finances, ideas, goals, and product roadmap. Each Sunday, she spent 90 minutes reviewing metrics: sales, email open rates, top-performing posts, and refund requests. If something wasn't working, she changed it. If something worked, she scaled it. There was no fluff—just quiet, deliberate action.

Lena also avoided the pressure to "look big." She didn't hire a virtual assistant. She didn't outsource her copywriting or video editing. If a task couldn't be done with AI or a drag-and-drop tool, she probably didn't need it. She used ElevenLabs to narrate her digital guides into short audio explainers, turned blog posts into Reels with Pictory, and used Canva to design everything from product mockups to pins. Her rule was simple: if she had to do it more than once, it needed to be automated or eliminated.

Six months in, Lena was making over $7,500/month from two products and a mini-course—all automated, all passive. Her daily operations took less than 90 minutes. She worked in her pajamas, often from a beach rental or coffee shop, and traveled often. Her customers thought she had a small team. She didn't correct them. The truth? Her only "employees" were ChatGPT, Make.com, and a well-organized Notion dashboard.

Lena's story isn't about avoiding hard work—it's about working with clarity. She didn't build a company in the traditional sense. She built a system. She designed a lifestyle that gave her peace, not pressure. And by embracing minimalism and letting AI do the heavy lifting, she proved something powerful: a one-person business can look, earn, and operate like a full enterprise—without the stress. No office. No team. No problem.

Chapter 7: How to Build a Global Brand From Home

In today's digital world, geography no longer limits opportunity. With the right systems, content, and tools, you can build a global brand from the comfort of your home—reaching customers across countries, cultures, and time zones. What used to take a marketing agency, a corporate PR team, and international partnerships can now be accomplished by one person with a clear message, a mobile phone, and AI. Building a global brand is no longer about scale—it's about clarity, consistency, and smart automation.

The first step is defining your brand identity. Who are you helping, and what transformation are you offering? A global brand doesn't try to be everything to everyone. It solves a specific problem for a clearly defined audience—and it does so in a way that feels personal. Start by writing a one-sentence brand promise: "I help [audience] achieve [result] using [method or approach]." For example: "I help beginner entrepreneurs build passive income streams using AI tools—without coding or startup capital." This brand clarity should appear across your content, bios, email signature, and product pages. Repetition builds recognition.

Next, choose your brand voice and design. AI tools like

ChatGPT can help you develop a tone guide for your messaging—formal, friendly, playful, or authoritative. Use Canva to create brand kits that include colors, fonts, logo variations, and visual styles. Consistent aesthetics across platforms (Instagram, LinkedIn, YouTube, newsletters) make your business memorable and professional, even if you're working solo from your kitchen table.

Now, translate your message into multiple content formats to reach people across languages, cultures, and platforms. Use ChatGPT or DeepL to translate your content into Spanish, French, or any other language relevant to your audience. If you have a course or product, record multilingual versions or add translated subtitles using tools like Kapwing or Subly. This immediately expands your market reach and positions your brand as international.

Lean into platforms that have global distribution. YouTube, for instance, is accessible in over 100 countries. Posting faceless AI-generated Shorts or long-form explainers lets you build trust at scale. Instagram Reels, TikTok, and Pinterest also have global reach and are perfect for visual storytelling. Every time someone shares, saves, or comments on your content, it opens new doors across borders. Use scheduling tools like Metricool to post across time zones and track global engagement.

To further expand your brand's global presence, build digital products that don't rely on location. Ebooks, prompt packs, templates, audio trainings, and Notion-based courses can be delivered instantly to anyone, anywhere. Use Gumroad, Payhip, or LemonSqueezy to accept payments globally and offer pricing in multiple currencies. This reduces purchase friction and boosts international conversions. Use Make.com to segment customers by country or language and send personalized post-purchase emails accordingly.

To support and engage your global audience, create community spaces. Build a private email newsletter, Telegram group, or Discord server. Use Notion or Skool to host a simple membership site where customers around the world can learn, ask questions, and connect. Keep the interface simple, clean, and mobile-friendly. AI can help moderate, answer FAQs, and translate messages so no one feels left out.

Establish credibility with global testimonials. Ask happy customers to record short video or text reviews. Use AI voice tools to narrate their testimonials in multiple languages, and embed them on your sales page. Add country flags or language tags to highlight the diversity of your customer base. When people from Brazil, India, France, or Canada see themselves represented, they trust your brand faster.

Finally, make your story part of your brand. Let people know that you're a one-person business using AI to build something real. Share behind-the-scenes looks at your systems, tools, and process. People don't just buy products—they buy stories. When they see you, at home, creating with purpose and serving a global audience, they're inspired. That inspiration turns into loyalty.

With the right messaging, automation, and content strategy, you can grow far beyond your zip code. You don't need a team, office, or advertising agency to be seen around the world. You just need a system, a story, and the willingness to show up consistently. The next chapter will guide you through scaling this brand into a six-figure machine—powered almost entirely by AI.

Clarity in Chaos

Amara lived in a small apartment in Nairobi, Kenya, where power outages and patchy internet were just part of her daily routine. She had studied marketing in college but struggled to land a traditional job after graduation. What she did have was a phone, a laptop, and a burning desire to create something of her own. She had always loved personal development and journaling, and during the lockdowns, she began posting motivational quotes and journaling prompts on Instagram.

Her posts were simple but heartfelt. Then one day, a stranger from Canada messaged her: "Do you sell these prompts as a product?"

That question sparked an idea. Amara spent the next week building her first digital product: a 30-day digital journal titled *Clarity in Chaos*. She used Canva to design it, ChatGPT to help write the prompts, and Gumroad to sell it. She priced it at $10. On the day she launched, she made a single sale—from someone in Australia. That tiny sale lit her up. She wasn't just creating content anymore. She was building a brand—and not just in Kenya, but around the world.

She leaned into her story. On her Instagram Reels, she showed behind-the-scenes clips of herself building her digital product during blackouts, working by candlelight, and recording voiceovers using ElevenLabs. She was honest, authentic, and deeply relatable. She shared how AI was helping her compete globally even though she didn't have a big budget or a fancy setup. Her content started getting shared—first by other African creators, then by international digital nomads. Her follower count began to rise.

Amara decided to turn her journal into a global product. She used DeepL and ChatGPT to translate it into Spanish and French. She added those versions to her Gumroad store and updated her landing page with international flags and translated product descriptions. Sales tripled. She started receiving messages from Argentina, Morocco, and Switzerland. People were amazed that someone from a remote part of the world was creating content they could relate to—and they wanted more.

She launched a free lead magnet: *7 Days of Guided Reflection,* translated into three languages. She used MailerLite to automate the delivery and nurture sequence. New subscribers were funneled into her digital product funnel, and after purchase, they were offered a $47 audio course narrated with an AI voice in their language of choice. Her income began to stabilize. Her brand went from an Instagram account to a global personal development hub—all built from her laptop, in her bedroom.

What made Amara's brand grow wasn't just the products—it was her presence. She showed up consistently, shared her story vulnerably, and used every AI tool available to remove language and tech barriers. She scheduled her content in advance using Metricool and tracked her growth in a Notion dashboard she designed herself. She turned her solo journey into a source of connection for thousands of people who felt seen and empowered through her message.

By month six, Amara had customers in over 40 countries and had generated over $8,000 in sales. She was invited to speak on virtual panels, guest-featured in blogs, and even interviewed on a podcast hosted in the U.K. She had become a global brand without ever leaving her city. And every part of her business—marketing, product creation, customer delivery—was powered by AI and smart systems.

Amara's story is a testament to what's possible today. You don't need connections. You don't need startup capital. You don't need perfect conditions. You just need the courage to start, the discipline to keep showing up, and the creativity to use the tools you have. With AI and authenticity, she built a brand that transcended borders—and so can you.

Chapter 8: Scaling to 6 Figures Using AI-Only Systems

Reaching $10K+ per month isn't about grinding harder—it's about scaling smarter. Once your first few digital products are selling, and your systems are running on autopilot, your next challenge is scaling that success into a six-figure income stream. Scaling doesn't mean doing more manually; it means improving what's already working, increasing reach, stacking revenue streams, and doubling down on automation. In this chapter, you'll learn how to use AI-powered systems to scale your one-person business to consistent, global income—without burning out or building a massive team.

The first step in scaling is refining your funnel. Look at your current lead magnet, email sequence, and product flow. Use analytics from ConvertKit, MailerLite, or Notion to identify drop-off points. Are people opening emails but not clicking? Clicking but not buying? Use ChatGPT to rewrite your subject lines, hooks, and CTAs. A single improved sequence can increase conversions by 20–50%. A/B test headlines, buttons, and offers. Scaling starts with optimizing what you already have, not launching something new every week.

Next, multiply your traffic sources. If you've been relying solely on organic traffic from one platform, expand to 2–3 more. Use your existing AI-written scripts to create short-form videos for Instagram, TikTok, and YouTube Shorts. Repurpose your blog posts into Twitter threads, LinkedIn articles, or Pinterest pins. Use Metricool to track what drives traffic and set up smart scheduling. You're not creating more—you're multiplying reach with what's already been created, using AI to format and post across multiple platforms.

Then, increase your product depth. Offer bundles, upsells, and subscriptions. AI can help you create tiered versions of the same product—a starter pack, a pro version, and a premium bundle. You can also create related products using existing frameworks. For example, turn a single ebook into an audio version, a printable version, a course, and a coaching guide. Use tools like ElevenLabs, Canva, and Notion to generate new formats in hours, not weeks. The more options people have to engage with your brand, the higher your average order value (AOV).

Another scaling strategy is affiliate marketing—either by becoming one or creating your own program. Promote AI tools you already use and trust, embedding affiliate links in your products, thank-you pages, and YouTube descriptions. Sign up for programs like Gumroad Discover, AppSumo, or PartnerStack. You can also let others promote your products. Set up an affiliate dashboard using Gumroad or Payhip and recruit micro-influencers in your niche. AI can help write outreach emails, design promotional graphics, and create swipe copy for your partners.

As your brand grows, expand globally with localization. Use AI tools like DeepL, ChatGPT, and Kapwing to translate and subtitle your content. Offer your most popular products in 2–3 additional languages. Use Notion or Google Sheets to track translation workflows and automate delivery with Make.com. This alone can double or triple your income without adding new products—just new audiences. AI lets you do this quickly and affordably, removing traditional barriers to global scale.

Finally, measure everything and make decisions based on data. Use a Notion dashboard to track KPIs: daily sales, conversion rates, top traffic sources, and refund rates. Every week, ask: what's working? What can be automated further? What needs to be improved? Scaling doesn't happen by accident—it's the result of consistent, strategic decisions powered by insight. AI can help analyze your data, suggest changes, and even implement improvements automatically through tools like Make.com.

To scale with sanity, remember: don't try to do everything at once. Choose one growth lever at a time—optimize a funnel, expand a traffic channel, increase average order value—and let your AI systems handle the rest. This chapter isn't about hustling more. It's about building smarter. The next chapter will take you one step further—ensuring that as you grow, your income is stable, secure, and ready for long-term sustainability.

Dev's Make.com story

Dev had always been entrepreneurial, but his side hustles never scaled. He had tried everything—drop shipping, freelancing, even launching a t-shirt brand—but each project hit a ceiling. Either it demanded too much time or couldn't grow past a few hundred dollars a month. Then he discovered AI tools and digital product automation. At first, he created a small Notion-based digital planner, enhanced with ChatGPT productivity prompts. He used Canva to design it, listed it on Gumroad for $19, and marketed it through a free lead magnet and short-form video content. The system worked—he started earning $1,200–$1,500 per month within six weeks. For the first time, Dev wasn't just making money online—he had built something that ran itself.

But Dev didn't stop there. He wanted to scale, and he knew that meant working smarter, not harder. He started by optimizing his funnel. Using Make.com, he built a smarter post-purchase sequence. After someone bought the planner, they received an upsell offer—an AI-generated content calendar bundled with bonus coaching prompts. The offer converted well, adding an extra $1,000 per month with zero extra content creation. He also used ChatGPT to rewrite his email series, improving click-through rates by nearly 40%. These small tweaks made a big difference.

Next, Dev looked at his traffic. Up until that point, most sales had come from Instagram. He decided to expand to YouTube Shorts and TikTok. Rather than start from scratch, he took his most successful scripts, tweaked them slightly, and used Invideo to generate new video versions. He batched 30 pieces of content in one weekend and scheduled them across platforms using Metricool. By month three, his reach had tripled. One short video about "how I made $2,000/month with a Notion planner and AI" went viral and brought in 400 new email subscribers in 48 hours.

Dev then expanded his product line—without starting from scratch. He turned the planner into an interactive Notion dashboard. Then he used ElevenLabs to narrate an audio walkthrough and added that to a premium version. He even used Tally to create a quiz called "What's Your Productivity Style?" that segmented leads into different follow-up sequences. People loved the personalized touch. Every quiz result ended with a product recommendation, and sales increased by 25% overnight.

To scale further, Dev created an affiliate program. Using Gumroad's built-in affiliate feature, he recruited other productivity creators to promote his planner. He used ChatGPT to write email templates, promo captions, and swipe copy. He didn't have to do any outreach—he simply posted about it in Notion communities and productivity groups. Within a few weeks, he had ten affiliates consistently driving traffic and earning commissions. His reach expanded into audiences he never would've found on his own.

Dev also began translating his products into Spanish and Hindi. He hired no one—just used ChatGPT and DeepL to write and ElevenLabs to record. He updated his product pages to reflect the new languages, added translated product previews, and created localized checkout experiences with LemonSqueezy. The response was incredible. International customers began pouring in, thanking him for making personal growth tools accessible to them. His audience grew, and his sales diversified.

By month six, Dev had hit $10,300 in monthly income—with no office, no team, and no burnout. Every system in his business was optimized. He had automated content, emails, product delivery, upsells, customer support, and even testimonials using AI prompts. His job had become one of oversight: checking dashboards, testing new ideas, and spending time learning instead of grinding. The best part? He still had his freedom. He worked 15 hours a week, mostly in the mornings, and spent his afternoons hiking, reading, and traveling.

Dev's journey from a stuck side hustler to a six-figure AI entrepreneur wasn't based on luck. It was built on systems—simple, repeatable, and scalable systems that AI helped him build piece by piece. He learned that you don't scale by adding chaos. You scale by refining what works, automating the rest, and letting AI multiply your effort. That mindset turned his small project into a global, six-figure digital business—and it can do the same for you.

Chapter 9: Sustainable Growth & Long-Term Exit Planning

Once your AI-powered business begins generating consistent revenue, it's time to think beyond daily sales and weekly goals. Sustainable growth means building a system that not only earns well now but continues to thrive in the future—whether you're running it, selling it, or stepping back from it. It means building assets instead of tasks, equity instead of just income. This chapter is about future-proofing your AI empire by designing it to scale sustainably and, eventually, become a sellable digital asset—without you in the driver's seat every day.

The first step is separating yourself from the day-to-day operations. If your business relies on your constant presence, you haven't yet built an asset—you've built a job. Begin documenting your systems and processes, even if you're a one-person show. Use Notion or Google Docs to create standard operating procedures (SOPs) for everything: how you create content, how products are delivered, how emails are scheduled, and how customer service is handled. These SOPs will serve two purposes: they'll help you delegate in the future if needed, and they'll increase your business's value if you choose to sell.

Then, systematize your growth strategies. Don't chase trends or constantly switch products. Instead, build product lines, bundles, and evergreen funnels that perform consistently. Use AI to analyze your best-performing content, email campaigns, and products. Double down on what works, and automate ongoing testing to refine it further. Use Make.com or Airtable to track customer lifetime value, acquisition costs, and churn rates. These aren't just metrics—they're levers for sustainable scale.

To maintain consistent revenue, implement recurring income streams. Instead of relying solely on one-time product sales, add subscriptions or memberships. These can include AI prompt clubs, digital download libraries, or behind-the-scenes content for your audience. Platforms like Gumroad, Patreon, and Memberstack allow you to deliver recurring value with minimal overhead. AI tools can help generate new content each month, update templates, or rotate lead magnets—all without your direct input.

As your systems grow stronger, build a moat—something that protects your business from competition and copycats. This can be your unique story, your community, proprietary frameworks, or even exclusive AI prompt libraries you've refined over time. Share insights that are hard to replicate. Build a recognizable brand that customers associate with trust and results. And if you're not ready to be public-facing, create a distinct brand name, aesthetic, and tone that can stand on its own—even without your face behind it.

Then, think like an investor. If you were going to buy your own business, what would you want to see? Recurring income, minimal overhead, automated systems, and a growing list of happy customers. Prepare your business as if you were selling it—even if you aren't. Track your monthly recurring revenue (MRR), total customer value, conversion rates, churn, and refunds. These metrics don't just help you optimize—they make your business more appealing to acquirers on platforms like Flippa, Acquire, or Empire Flippers.

You can also consider licensing. If you've created successful AI-powered products, you can license them to others—either under your brand or as white-label products. For example, if you've built an AI content prompt library for coaches, license it to business mentors who can rebrand and sell it as their own. Licensing lets you earn income without more work—and it increases the reach of your original product.

Finally, protect your time, your energy, and your systems. Growth doesn't mean working more hours—it means refining your systems to work better. Build a weekly CEO routine where you analyze your dashboard, update your goals, and assess what can be automated further. Ask yourself regularly: "If I disappeared for a month, would this business keep growing?" If the answer is yes, you've built a scalable asset. If not, use that awareness to guide your next upgrade.

Sustainable growth is about freedom—time freedom, financial freedom, and eventually, freedom of choice. Whether you choose to continue scaling, sell for a lump sum, or simply enjoy the passive income you've created, the foundation is the same: clear systems, recurring revenue, and intelligent use of AI. The final chapter will walk you through wrapping up your empire with long-term clarity—so your business can grow with or without you.

Eli and the Creator Vault

Eli never thought he would build a business worth selling. What started as a way to make ends meet during a rough patch in his life turned into a thriving six-figure digital brand powered by AI, Notion dashboards, and clever automations. For two years, he sold AI content tools for freelance writers, ran a small membership for digital creators, and created content that reached tens of thousands of people every month. But as life changed—he got married, started thinking about moving abroad, and wanted more time offline—he began asking a new question: what would it look like to step away?

He started preparing without telling anyone. He opened a clean Notion workspace labeled "Exit Ready" and began documenting everything. His product workflows, his email sequences, how he scheduled content, how refunds were processed, how customer questions were handled—all written clearly and simply. He included links, walkthroughs, templates, and even Loom videos to explain the logic behind certain automations. The goal wasn't just to sell. It was to make the business run beautifully without him.

Eli then took inventory. He noticed that 85% of his income came from two core products and one membership. So, he focused on optimizing those. He rewrote his evergreen email sequences using ChatGPT, retested his top five lead magnets, and rebuilt his upsell pages to match current trends. Sales increased by 22% in 30 days. Next, he created a system where new subscribers would be tagged based on what lead magnet they came through, and automatically funneled into tailored product offers. He didn't write the emails himself—AI did most of the work.

To increase recurring income, Eli bundled his top digital downloads into a $9/month subscription called *The Creator Vault*. He used Gumroad for delivery, Canva for promotion, and Make.com to rotate new content into the vault automatically each month. He then added upsell offers to convert subscribers into lifetime members for $97. This added consistency to his income and made the business more attractive to potential buyers.

By month four of preparing his exit, Eli realized he had unintentionally doubled his business valuation—without launching anything new. His growth came not from expansion, but from refinement. With ChatGPT and Airtable, he even created a monthly dashboard that forecasted revenue based on subscriber churn, average order value, and recent trends. He felt like a real CEO for the first time—one who understood his numbers and had the power to improve them with a few adjustments.

Eventually, he listed his business on Acquire.com. He included all assets: Notion documentation, AI tools used, templates, customer lists, and future product ideas. His pitch was simple: "A one-person AI-powered digital product business with documented systems, predictable revenue, and passive fulfillment." Within two weeks, he had three serious offers. He chose a buyer who wanted to maintain the brand, and they agreed on a $110,000 cash sale with a 60-day handoff period. Eli had created, scaled, and sold a fully digital, AI-powered brand—without employees, ads, or traditional infrastructure.

He walked away with more than money. He had time, clarity, and a blueprint he could repeat again if he ever chose to. And maybe he would. But for now, he was off to Spain with his wife and his laptop, knowing that the skills and systems he'd developed would serve him for life. He hadn't just built income—he had built a sellable asset. And all of it began with a few AI tools and a decision to stop hustling and start building something real.

Eli's journey proves that sustainability isn't about slowing down. It's about scaling smart, building systems, and keeping your future options open. Whether you sell, automate, or simply coast into a four-hour workweek, the empire you've built becomes your launchpad for whatever comes next.

Chapter 10: The Long-Term Vision: Freedom, Leverage, and Legacy

Reaching six figures with an AI-powered business is an incredible milestone—but it's only the beginning. The true reward of building a lean, automated, global business isn't just the income—it's the freedom that comes with it. Time freedom. Location freedom. Creative freedom. And eventually, legacy. In this final chapter, we'll zoom out and look at how to evolve your business beyond survival and even beyond success. You'll learn how to turn your systems into a platform for long-term impact, reinvest in your freedom, and leave behind something bigger than a product or brand—something that lasts.

First, let's talk about freedom. Most people start online businesses to earn extra income or quit their job. But over time, if you're not intentional, you can recreate the same stress and time traps you were trying to escape. The antidote is intentional design. Build your weeks around how you want to live, not just how much you want to earn. Use your calendar to protect "freedom blocks" of non-work time. Let automation handle fulfillment, lead generation, and onboarding. Use AI to replace unnecessary tasks and decision-making. You are not just your business—you're its architect. Build it to serve your life, not the other way around.

Next, think in terms of leverage. Every piece of content, automation, or digital product you create is an asset that can be used over and over again. That's the essence of leverage—doing the work once and getting paid for it forever. Stack leverage by building product ecosystems: ebooks lead to courses, courses lead to memberships, memberships lead to affiliates. Every touchpoint compounds your brand value. Use AI to maintain this machine—repurposing, refreshing, and optimizing your assets instead of constantly starting over.

Now consider your platform. You've likely built an audience, even if it's small. A newsletter, a community, a group of followers who trust you. That's powerful. Use this platform to elevate others, create collaborations, and even incubate new creators. You can create guest courses, host workshops, or partner on bundles. You can launch micro-brands under your umbrella or license your systems to others. What started as a one-person side hustle can become a digital ecosystem that supports others while continuing to grow.

Then there's reinvestment. Once your business is generating steady income, start redirecting that money into assets that secure your long-term freedom. This could include buying income-producing digital products from others, investing in real estate, or launching a new SaaS product using your existing audience. You don't need to scale forever. You just need to shift from "earned income" to "owner income." Use your profits to buy time, peace, and security. The earlier you think like an investor, the faster you build wealth beyond work.

Finally, there's legacy. What are you really building? What will outlast the platforms, trends, and algorithms? Your legacy is the combination of the systems you've created, the people you've helped, and the values you've embodied. Document your story. Teach others what you've learned. Package your process. Whether you sell your business, license your frameworks, or write a book, your journey can live on as a guide for others. That's the most powerful form of passive income—impact that continues long after you've stepped away.

To build an empire isn't to build something huge—it's to build something meaningful, self-sustaining, and deeply aligned with the life you want. AI has given you the tools. You've now built the system. The final move is vision: choosing how you want to use the power, freedom, and influence you've created. Whether you continue growing, exit, or shift into something new, you now have the skills, systems, and leverage to do it on your terms.

This book may be ending—but your journey is just beginning. In the final story chapter, you'll hear how one creator took everything they built and turned it into a life of purpose, peace, and global impact—without ever returning to the hustle.

Sophia's new stable income

Sophia was no stranger to reinvention. She had spent the better part of two decades chasing stability—first as a high school teacher, then as a freelance curriculum developer, and finally as a digital course creator. When the AI boom started gaining traction, she was quick to adapt. She learned how to use ChatGPT, Notion, and Pictory. She built a suite of products—ebooks, AI prompt packs, and mini-courses for educators—and gradually grew her business into a lean, profitable machine. Within two years, she was earning over $12,000 a month and working less than 20 hours a week. But as her systems stabilized, a new question emerged: What now?

Sophia found herself waking up without urgency. Her business was running smoothly. Emails were answered by a chatbot. Sales came in regularly. Her team? A dashboard of automations and AI integrations. She had won the freedom she had always wanted—but something felt incomplete. She wasn't chasing money anymore; she was searching for meaning. And so, she began to think bigger. Not in terms of scale, but in terms of impact.

She started hosting small group Zoom calls—not to sell, but to teach. She opened up about her process: how she used AI, how she structured her weeks, how she overcame fear. These sessions were raw and real, and people connected with her deeply. Soon, she created a mentorship circle where she helped others build their own AI-powered income streams. She charged a modest fee, more to encourage commitment than to profit. The program filled quickly—not because she marketed it hard, but because she had become a trusted guide.

Sophia also began licensing her materials. She created a white-label version of her educator AI prompt packs and allowed coaches and consultants to rebrand and resell them. Her products were now earning her income from people she had never met, in industries she had never worked in. What had started as digital worksheets had become revenue-generating assets scattered across the internet—owned by others, but built by her.

With her income stable and her time her own, she began investing. Not in flashy things, but in security. She bought a small plot of land outside of the city. She renovated a cottage. She planted fruit trees. And she set up a simple solar system to power her home. Her days became slower but fuller—writing in the mornings, mentoring in the afternoons, reading in the evenings. She didn't need more. She had enough.

But Sophia wasn't done. She decided to write a book—not a how-to, but a memoir of sorts. She called it *Built With Peace*. It told the story of how she escaped burnout, built a life-first business, and used AI not as a crutch but as a partner in her creative evolution. She self-published, narrated the audiobook using ElevenLabs, and donated a portion of sales to literacy projects. The book didn't go viral, but it resonated. Dozens of emails poured in—messages from mothers, burned-out teachers, remote workers—each one saying, "This is what I've been looking for."

One evening, as the sun set over her quiet backyard, Sophia opened her laptop. She checked her sales dashboard—not out of anxiety, but habit. Everything was humming along. She smiled, closed the lid, and looked out at the trees swaying in the breeze. She had built a business. She had built systems. But more importantly, she had built a life—a life on her terms, with time to rest, space to think, and the ability to help others rise.

Sophia's story is the final proof that your empire doesn't have to be loud or massive to matter. It needs to be intentional. It needs to be aligned with your values. And it needs to give you not just income—but peace, leverage, and the chance to leave something behind. With AI as your partner and vision as your compass, the next chapter is entirely up to you.

Epilogue: The New Blueprint: Rise of the One-Person Empire

We've reached the end of this book, but the most important part of your journey is just beginning. The chapters you've listened to weren't just strategies and stories. They were blueprints—small windows into what's now possible in a world transformed by artificial intelligence. For the first time in history, it's no longer just the wealthy, the connected, or the credentialed who have the tools to build global, profitable, impactful businesses. Anyone with curiosity, consistency, and a Wi-Fi connection can now build an empire from a kitchen table, a coffee shop, or a corner of their bedroom.

What used to take a staff of ten, a $100,000 budget, and years of trial and error can now be built by one person in months—sometimes weeks. AI doesn't just make business faster. It makes freedom more accessible. It removes the need for permission. It turns the knowledge in your head—and the tools in your browser—into real income, real assets, and real transformation for both you and the people you serve.

But with this power comes a responsibility: to use it wisely. It's tempting to chase everything. More platforms. More tools. More launches. But real success lies in focus, simplicity, and alignment. Choose a niche that excites you. Build a product that solves a real problem. Use automation to deliver consistent value. Show up for your audience. Refine your systems. Protect your time. And never forget why you started—freedom, impact, peace, or the ability to be present in your life.

You've now seen how to go from idea to income. From product to platform. From scattered hustle to a global, automated, AI-powered brand. You've met creators who built six-figure businesses with no team, no ads, and no investors—just smart systems, clear offers, and intentional execution. They didn't do anything magical. They followed the roadmap. And now, so can you.

As you move forward, you don't need to build it all at once. Start with one idea. One product. One platform. Let AI amplify your creativity, not replace it. Let automation give you space, not distance you from your audience. Let leverage become your strategy, not your shortcut. The journey of building your empire is iterative—and every system you build compounds.

Remember, the goal isn't just money. It's design. It's control. It's creating a life where your business works for you, not the other way around. Whether you choose to scale, sell, simplify, or start something new, the skills you've gained here are permanent. You now know how to build income without trading time. How to grow without hiring. How to impact thousands without burnout. That's leverage. That's power. That's freedom.

And if someday you wake up and decide to take a month off, to relocate, to raise a family, or to build something completely different—you can. Because you've built systems. Because your income isn't dependent on being busy. Because your brand runs without you constantly showing up. That's the essence of a one-person empire: it's sustainable. It's scalable. It's optional.

So as you close this book, ask yourself: what is the next step I can take in the next 24 hours? Can I draft a lead magnet? Can I outline my first product? Can I automate my first email? Can I launch a landing page? Don't wait until everything is perfect. Start. Build momentum. Adjust as you grow.

There's a new economy rising—and it's not run by institutions or agencies. It's run by creators, solopreneurs, educators, and problem solvers who are leveraging AI to serve at scale. You are now one of them. Whether your empire earns $1,000 a month or $100,000, it belongs to you. Built with your ideas. Powered by your systems. And aligned with your purpose.

This isn't the end. It's the handoff—from this book to your action. You're ready. Your tools are ready. The market is ready.

Now it's time to build, grow, and live like the empire was already yours—because now, it is.

www.ingramcontent.com/pod-product-compliance
Lightning Source LLC
LaVergne TN
LVHW022021200926
848481LV00007B/2477